PUEBLO INDIAN

by STEVEN CORY

ILLUSTRATIONS BY RICHARD ERICKSON

LERNER PUBLICATIONS COMPANY
MINNEAPOLIS, MINNESOTA

The American Pastfinder series is produced by Lerner Publications Company in cooperation with Greenleaf Publishing, Inc., St. Charles, Illinois.

Design by Melanie Lawson

Cory, Steven.
    Pueblo Indian / by Steven Cory ; illustrations by Richard Erickson.
        p. cm. — (American pastfinder)
    Includes index.
    ISBN 0-8225-2976-9 (alk. paper)
    1. Pueblo Indians—History—Juvenile literature. 2. Pueblo Indians—
Social life and customs—Juvenile literature. [1. Pueblo Indians. 2. Indians of
North America.] I. Erickson, Richard (Richard W.), ill. II. Title. III.
Series.
E99.P9C768 1996
973'.04974—dc20   95-3739

Manufactured in the United States of America
1 2 3 4 5 6 - H - 01 00 99 98 97 96

Contents

INTRODUCTION

On a cold December day in 1888, two cowboys were rounding up cattle near the Mancos River in Colorado. They had often chased strays through the maze of canyons and hills. But this time they chanced upon something astonishing. They found themselves staring at a large group of stone houses and towers tucked into the side of a massive cliff. After struggling up to the buildings with makeshift ladders, they entered a site forgotten for centuries. Inside the buildings they found skeletal remains, pots, an axe, and other things that would have been left behind only by people who were in a great hurry.

The cowboys had stumbled upon the famous Cliff Palace of Mesa Verde, only one of many long-abandoned stone cities found in present-day Colorado, Arizona, and New Mexico. We will probably never know for certain why the inhabitants had to leave. But we can admire their well-crafted buildings and relics—pottery, carvings, petroglyphs (drawings on stone)—of a culture that flourished centuries before white people came to America. Modern-day Indians call the builders of these ancient cities the Anasazi, the "ancient ones." A more familiar name for this group is Pueblo.

5

CENTURIES OF CULTURE

Some people think of early Native Americans—American Indians—as nomads, constantly on the move, pitching their tepees wherever their search for game took them. But not all Native American peoples lived this way—and certainly not the Pueblo Indians. The term *pueblo* is simply the Spanish word for "town." The Spaniards gave this name to a diverse group of Indian tribes because they all lived in settled communities.

Historians believe that people have lived in the American Southwest for more than 12,000 years. These early human inhabitants did not have a settled life. They struggled to keep themselves fed in ways we find almost unimaginable. With weapons made only of wood, stone, and bone, they attacked and killed gigantic mammoths, woolly rhinoceroses, and long-necked camels. At that time the Southwest was a region of forests and swamps. But between 6,000 and 8,000 years ago, the area dried up and became the desert it is today. The great beasts became extinct. People who continued to live in the Southwest had to find a new way of life.

The Cochise people, the next group to live in the region, did just that. They hunted smaller prey—deer, rabbit, snakes, and lizards. They foraged for wild plants—berries, nuts, beans, and cactus. Such hunters and gatherers needed to travel constantly in small bands to survive. But about 5,000 years ago, the Cochise began to plant corn and other crops. Farming led to a more settled life and the first houses—pits dug into the earth with an entrance tunnel, a roof of branches and wood, and a fire pit in the middle.

The Cochise gradually gave way to the Mogollon culture. These people also built pit houses, but they were the first to arrange the houses in towns, with a large house in the center as a meeting place for religious events. They tamed dogs and turkeys and made pipes for smoking, which was a sacred rite.

The people of the Hohokam culture lived at the same time as the Mogollon peoples and gradually came to outnumber them. The Hohokam built houses out of wooden beams covered with mud. To bring water to their crops, they built irrigation systems—networks of canals that eventually covered more than 150 miles. The Hohokam also had time to make things of beauty, including lovely ornaments and cosmetic boxes.

Around 2,000 years ago, the "Basket Maker" culture began to develop alongside the Mogollon and Hohokam. These people were the first Anasazi, the "ancient ones," who left pictures on stone that we can still see today. They learned to plant corn and squash and hunted in groups with nets. Their houses were dome shaped and built of sticks covered with mud. They wove intricate baskets, wore many types of jewelry, and the men especially wore elaborate hairdos.

Beginning around A.D. 700, the Anasazi, or Pueblo people, built the cities we can still visit today. These cities are also called pueblos. The Anasazi were skillful at surviving in a hot, dry climate. Still, it seems that a drought between 1276 and 1299 forced people to abandon many of the settlements. Another period of depopulation occurred around 1450.

By the time the Spaniards arrived in 1540, the number of Pueblo people had greatly declined. But the culture—the customs, beliefs, and arts of the people—still thrived. This culture continues into the present, even though Pueblo people have often been oppressed, enslaved, and even killed since the arrival of Europeans in the American Southwest. Among the Pueblo tribes surviving today are the Hopi, the Keres, the Tewa, and the Zuni. About 30 Pueblo villages are still populated. There are important differences between these peoples—they speak many different languages, for example—but there are also remarkable similarities.

Looking Back in Time

Like the sands of Egypt, which preserved many artifacts of the ancient Egyptian culture, the desert of the Southwest causes things to dry out. Pottery, buildings, scraps of clothing, and even human remains that would have rotted and disappeared long ago in other climates have survived there. Archaeologists, people who study the remains of past cultures, have a lot of clues that help them reconstruct ancient Pueblo life.

When digging up an ancient site, archaeologists often find layers of artifacts, piled one on top of the other. Over time, people often rebuilt homes and even whole towns on top of a pile of rubbish from an older home that had fallen into disrepair. In archaeology, the deeper down you go, the older things are.

Telling Time with Tree Rings and Pottery

Another sort of helpful layering is found in pieces of wood. Slice through a tree trunk and you will see many rings. Each ring represents the amount of wood the tree added to itself during one year. A fat ring usually means there was good rainfall that year, while a thin ring resulted from a dry year. The series of thin, fat, and middle-sized rings makes a pattern that will be the same in all trees from a certain place and time. By cutting down a tree living today and noting where its rings match the pattern of a wooden beam cut at an earlier time, and then going from there to a still earlier piece of wood, and so on, archaeologists have been able to come up with tree-ring calendars that go back as far as the first century A.D. When a beam or supporting timber is found in the ruins of a Pueblo building, scientists can look at the pattern of the rings and determine when it was built.

Over the centuries, Pueblo Indians and their neighbors experimented with many different techniques for making and decorating their pots. At different times, different decorative patterns were in fashion. An archaeologist who has learned a lot about Pueblo pottery through the ages can look at pottery pieces and tell when they were made.

Archaeologists take special care when digging up ancient Pueblo sites, because they are uncovering not just ancient history, but the roots of a Pueblo culture that continues to this day. In some cases, archaeologists have left sites undisturbed, out of respect for the traditions and beliefs of the Pueblo people.

The Pueblo World

M any modern-day Americans pack up all their belongings and move several times in their lives. You probably won't live your whole life in the same place your parents lived. But Pueblo Indians preferred to stay in one place. They considered the land on which they lived to be an essential part of themselves.

The land where the ancient Pueblo Indians lived contains dry, searing hot desert and flat-topped hills called mesas. The region has strong winds, hot days, and cold nights. Finding enough water is a constant problem. What rain does fall gets absorbed by the claylike soil, and many rivers are dry for much of the year. In many areas, no humans have been able to survive since the Anasazi left, five centuries ago.

Yet this land is also a region of great beauty and has been called the "wonderland of America." The canyons of the Southwest, including the Grand Canyon, are spectacular. The mountains and deserts have a rugged splendor. In such an area, people must work hard to survive. With scarce water and small amounts of land for growing crops, farming requires great effort and care. Pueblo Indians were also very skilled at finding wild berries and nuts, and at hunting in an area where game was scarce.

Major Pueblo Sites

Utah

Colorado

Mesa Verde

Canyon de Chelly

Aztec

Taos

Hopi

Bandelier

Santa Fe

Chaco Canyon

Pecos

Flagstaff

Albuquerque

Acoma

Arizona

New Mexico

Phoenix

Casa Grande

Mimbres

● Pueblo
○ Major City

Living with Animals

When white people came to the land of the Pueblos and found a large population of rattlesnakes, they began killing them as dangerous pests. The Pueblos were horrified! To them, rattlesnakes—like tarantulas scorpions, and mountain lions—were not dangerous enemies but rather neighbors, part of the land. In fact, during the course of a year, some Indians collected rattlesnakes for a special ceremony, in which they danced with the snakes.

THE STORY OF CREATION

Like people all over the world, the Pueblos told and still tell stories that explain momentous events in the history of their culture. Such stories are a way for people to talk about what is important to them—the meaning of their lives and why they live the way they do. Perhaps the most important myth the Pueblos tell is the story of creation. The story has been told, and still is being told, in many different ways. Here is one version:

After creating the world, Tawa, the great God, planted living creatures— ants, beetles, and other things that crawl—deep inside the earth. Tawa told them how to live in peace with each other, but they couldn't understand, and so fought and quarreled. So Tawa sent Spider Grandmother to lead them up, closer to the earth's surface. And as they climbed, some found themselves transformed into larger animals—wolves, rabbits, coyotes.

But still they could not live according to Tawa's rules. So Tawa sent Spider Grandmother again, and she led the creatures to a world just below the surface of the earth. Here some became humans, and Spider Grandmother taught them to plant crops, to worship the gods, and to live in peace. But after some time most of the people fell under the influence of evil sorcerers. They became lazy and neglected their work. They stopped worshiping. They began fighting with each other.

A few of the people, however, kept the peaceful ways of Tawa. Tawa sent Spider Grandmother to bring them to the surface of the world. They and many animals emerged through a sipapu, a small hole in the earth. Once out of the ground, they founded the various civilizations of humankind.

This story reveals the Pueblos' belief that they are strongly connected to the earth, which is their place of origin. But at the same time, the story shows that they are proud to have risen above the world of animals, to have built a civilization. The Pueblos think of various canyons and craters as *sipapus*, places where the spirit world can enter into their lives. They also construct their own sipapus, covered holes that are part of their worship ceremonies.

Pueblo Indians strive to live in harmony with the earth, to work hard, and to act kindly toward each other. Pueblos think of themselves as living halfway between heaven and earth.

BUILDING A PUEBLO

*We build our houses like we make pottery, with our
bare hands and layers upon layers of wet earth.*

—a modern Pueblo Indian

Pueblo towns are somewhat like modern apartment buildings. Both are
clusters of small dwellings that share walls and floors. But there is an
important difference. Modern apartment-dwelling families decorate
and furnish their individual homes and spend a lot of their time shut
off from the outside world. But the pueblo is designed for community life.
Most of the homes face a common courtyard. Roofs become reserved
seating for the many ceremonies and celebrations that the people share.

In 1900 a visitor watched as a Pueblo woman built a house:

> With a small heap of adobe mud the woman, using her hand as a
> trowel, fills in the chinks, smooths and plasters the walls inside and
> out. Splashed from head to foot with mud, she is an object to
> behold, and, if her children are there to "help" her, no mudlarks
> ever looked more happy…. Then, when the whitewashing is
> done with gypsum [a chalky mineral], or the coloring of the
> walls, what fun the children have—as they splash their tiny
> hands into the coloring matter and dash it upon the walls.

During construction, religious leaders performed
ceremonies to protect the home from harm. They
hung special prayer feathers from the rafters and
sprinkled cornmeal on the floor while singing a
house-building song.

Digging and Mixing Adobe

The material for building their homes lay right at the
Pueblos' feet. A special kind of earth called "adobe"—
a mixture of clay and sand—covers much of the
American Southwest. Adobe is not much good for
farming, but it works great as a building material.
When mixed with water, it is easy to mold. For
extra strength, ashes, rocks, or straw are added.
Adobe also insulates, keeping Pueblo homes
warm in the winter and cool in the summer.

Roofing

Roofs are difficult to build out of stones or bricks, and Pueblo Indians did not have tools for hewing beams. So they devised a five-layer roofing method: first came poles, covered by thick sticks, then willow branches, then mud, and finally dry earth. These roofs supported the weight of many people and often became the floor of the apartment above.

Women's Work

In Pueblo society women took on many responsibilities, such as building houses and ovens and making pottery and baskets. Men generally did the farming and hunting and performed most of the spiritual rituals. In addition, men were expert weavers, knitters, and embroiderers.

LADDERS AND HATCHES

When some of the Pueblo cliff dwellings were discovered during the last century, visitors found they could reach them only after building complicated ladders and scaffolds. But the Anasazi had been able to climb up to these places using small handholds and footholds chiseled into the rocks—even while carrying heavy loads. Getting around in many Pueblo villages required athletic ability far greater than that needed to climb a staircase.

When the Spanish first saw pueblos, they were reminded of fortresses—difficult to get into and with few windows. In designing their villages, Pueblo Indians had in mind the possibility of sudden attack by enemies. So entryways were small, and ladders were collapsible.

Pueblo Indians had special prayers and ceremonies to ask the gods to protect their children on stairways and ladders. The stairs were only about a foot wide and did not have handrails. The ladders, made to be easily moved or taken apart, were sometimes unstable.

Hatches

There were no doorways on the first floor of an adobe home. Instead, people used enlarged windows. Upper floors were entered through hatches in the floor. "Up the ladder and down the ladder" is a Zuni expression meaning to enter a house. During rainstorms, the hatch could be covered with a large stone slab.

Type of Ladders

The notched log is an ancient ladder design, but was still in use in the 1880s. Sometimes a double ladder was used in high traffic areas, so one person could go down while another climbed.

A Pueblo Home

Pueblo homes measured about 12 by 20 feet—about one and a half times the size of a modern bedroom. Pueblo people were shorter and slimmer than we are today, and they spent most of their time out of doors. So they did not mind living in small quarters.

Only the Bare Essentials

A collection of rugs or animal skins served as a family bed at night. In the morning they were rolled up and used for seating. There were no tables or chairs. Wherever possible, space was conserved. Ledges were built into the walls, and storage bins for food were sometimes built into the floor. Pegs and poles suspended like towel racks were used for hanging what little clothing the people had. The fireplace snugged against one corner of the room and next to it could be found the cooking pots. Gourds—pumpkinlike vegetables—were dried, hollowed out, and used for carrying water. Every home had a trough for grinding corn.

Neat and Clean

The floor of a Pueblo home was either stone or packed earth, but Pueblo people were able to keep it very clean using brooms made from long strands of grass tied together. Walls were usually whitewashed, a process that takes much more time than painting. Gypsum had to be dug up and pounded into small pieces with a stone, then combined with cattle dung and baked like pottery. Finally, the mix was ground to a powder, combined with water, and smeared on the walls.

A Door or a Window?

The Pueblos didn't make a clear distinction between doors and windows. If a home had no entry hatch, people crawled through what we would today call a window. Before glass was introduced in the 1880s, Pueblos used selenite—a clear form of gypsum—as a window covering. In cold weather, the windows would sometimes be closed with adobe. Entryways were often made in a T shape, to make it easy for a person to enter while carrying something on his or her back.

THE CORN GROWERS

Treat your corn lovingly as you would treat your child.
    —an old Pueblo saying

Corn held a central place in Pueblo culture. Many stories recount how corn was given to the people, and when Pueblos wanted to ask favors of the gods, they usually offered corn. Pueblo Indians depended on corn for food. Without fields of this crop, they could not have settled in permanent villages.

In time, the Pueblos learned to cultivate other crops, especially cotton, pumpkins, beans, and peaches. Eagles and turkeys were raised, mostly for their feathers, which were braided into surprisingly warm blankets and used in religious ceremonies. After the coming of Europeans, Pueblos raised sheep, cattle, horses, goats, and chickens. Pueblo communities grew to include cultivated fields, corrals, and orchards. Planting, hoeing, and harvesting were done by large family groups, with everyone pitching in.

The Pueblos' wooden cultivating tools could not turn the earth over as well as a plow could, but this was actually a good thing. In Pueblo country, the few plots of ground that could grow crops were places where an underground water source provided moisture, a foot or so below the surface. The dried clay on the surface—which a normal plow would dig up—protected this water from drying up in the sun's heat. Pueblo farmers left the upper crust alone and poked holes to plant seeds deep down, where the moisture was.

A Pueblo Planting Prayer:

Mother, Father, you who belong to the great Beings,
you who belong to the Storm Clouds, you will help me.
I am ready to put down yellow corn and also blue corn.
Therefore you will help me and you will make my work light.
Also you will make the field not hard. You will make it soft.

A Thirsty Crop

Water was a constant concern. The Pueblo people performed special rain ceremonies and dances and spoke special prayers for rain. And they used great ingenuity to catch and hold the rains that might come just once a year. They built irrigation systems, using fiber mats to control the flow, sending water to just the right places. They dug pools—as large as 110 feet across and 4 feet deep—and lined them with masonry to hold rainwater. Sometimes people even got together in the winter and rolled huge snowballs down mountains and into the pools.

DRYING, GRINDING, AND COOKING

Fill your stomach and your face will brighten.
—an old Pueblo proverb

After the harvest, the Pueblo people sun-dried all sorts of fruits and vegetables, spreading them on roofs, hanging them from beams, poles, and even ladders. Ears of corn were braided—tied together by the husks—and hung wherever the sun could reach them. After storing these foods, mostly in dark chambers sealed off from rats and mice, the Pueblos were ready for winter.

Preparing the Corn

Dried corn keeps for a long time, but it is difficult to cook. The Pueblo people had almost 40 ways of cooking corn—most of which required that the corn first be ground into flour. To keep the household well supplied, a Pueblo woman had to grind corn for three to four hours every day. She did it with a set of three *metates* (grinding stones), arranged in a trough. After stripping corn from the ear, she ground the kernels on the roughest stone. Then the process was repeated with the next two stones, each smoother than the last. The resulting flour could be used to make dumplings, tamales, or *piki* (pee-kee), a wafer bread that would keep for a week. Piki could be cooked in the home, on a sort of griddle (see page 42 for a simple recipe). The regular morning drink was a gruel made by dropping loose cornmeal into boiling water. Large "beehive" ovens (shown through window, *right*) were used to bake round loaves of bread.

Rocky mountain bee plants

Broad-leaved yucca

Pine Nuts

Making "Sugar"

Today we use a chemical process to extract corn syrup, a sweetener, from corn. Pueblos did much the same thing, using saliva as the chemical. Their method was to have young girls chew fine cornmeal—after cleaning their mouths for days ahead of time with a special root. As the girls chewed, their saliva combined with the cornstarch to make a sweetener used in cooking.

Wild Crops

Pueblos gathered hundreds of wild plants, including foods much like potatoes, carrots, lettuce, spinach, mushrooms, and celery. Wild herbs gave them many seasonings. Mostly for ceremonial and religious purposes, Pueblo Indians smoked a mixture of herbs or barks. They used clay pipes or wrapped the mixture in corn husks. If a boy smoked before he had proved himself a skilled hunter, he was dunked in a river.

23

Clothes and Hairstyles

Early Anasazi wore clothing made of bark and grass. They tied turkey feathers and the skins of small animals together to make blankets. While most Native Americans wore animal skins, the Pueblos learned to grow cotton and weave it into beautiful clothing. By A.D. 800, most Pueblo people were wearing some cotton garments.

The Pueblos were skilled weavers. Contact with white people brought western-style sewing and fastening techniques, a greater variety of colors, and new cloths such as wool.

One popular hairstyle, often used by both men and women, was the "terrace" style: bangs in front, hair below the ear on the sides, and long hair in back. For ceremonies, women let their hair hang freely, but men's hair was elaborately dressed.

Early Pueblo dress consisted of simple pieces of cloth that were wrapped around the body and tied or tucked. There were no sleeves or pant legs, no buttons—in fact, no sewing. Men wore a strip wide enough to reach from waist to knee. Women wore long pieces of cloth, wrapped around their bodies like shawls. One shoulder was left bare.

Young women interested in finding a husband wore a special "butterfly" hairstyle, tied with two pieces of corn husk.

Moccasins appeared in the 1300s and soon replaced sandals made from yucca plants. For most Native Americans, the moccasin was something like a slipper. Only peoples of the Arctic and the Southwest wore shoes that reached above the ankle.

POTS AND BASKETS

Pottery and basket-making have been with the Pueblo people since the earliest times and have changed over many thousands of years. Different tribes, towns, and individuals expressed themselves with different techniques, shapes, and designs. Women made nearly all the pots and baskets.

The potter first had to dig up the clay, which was usually found in high mesas under slabs of rock. The clay was then soaked in water and mixed with ground-up stones or small pieces of broken pottery, to give added strength.

Once shaped, the pot would be dried in the sun and polished with stones until nearly glass smooth. Then it was whitewashed and painted with dyes made from ground-up rocks and water. Finally, the pot was ready for firing. It was placed in a pit and covered with old broken pieces of pottery to hold the heat. Then dry manure was shoveled into the pit and lit. The resulting fire was much hotter than burning wood. After two or three hours, the pot was strong and gleaming with color.

Pueblo basketry included trays, bowls, large containers for storing food, and gathering baskets with woven straps or handles. Some baskets were woven so closely that they could hold water. Dyes came from berries, flowers, clay, and rock.

Pueblos learned to make baskets of great strength, and they applied some basket-making techniques to the building of homes. Fibers from the yucca plant were used to lash beams together. Chimneys were basically tall "baskets" smeared with mud and clay.

Shaping Pots

Potters used two techniques for shaping pots. One technique started with a round lump of clay. The potter made an indentation in the center and progressively pushed out, rotating the clay as she shaped the piece with her fingers. The other technique was the coil method. Clay was rolled into long "snakes." These were stacked in spirals to create walls. In both cases, the potter smoothed the pots with carved scraping tools made from pieces of gourd. The pots were scraped until the walls were a uniform thickness.

TALKING WITH PICTURES

Petroglyphs—drawings carved on rocks—
are scattered throughout the Southwest.
Similar kinds of drawings are found on
old pottery. Modern-day Indians call these
pictures "writings." They seem to have been
drawn not just for decoration but also to transmit
information or tell a story. Some archaeologists
have attempted to find out what these talking
pictures mean. Not everyone agrees on the
translations, but they give an idea of what the
ancient Indians might have been trying to say.

Here's what some individual
characters may mean:

cloud

river

death

divided

rows of
crops

lightning

rainbow

snake

Messages on Bowls

Put symbols together and whole messages are created. The design on this bowl tells us: "Two pueblos are divided by war."

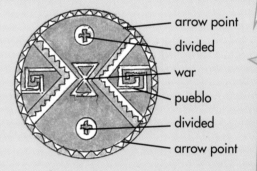

arrow point
divided
war
pueblo
divided
arrow point

The design on this pot tells us that, "Far away, across the land and under the clouds, there are two villages. One is large, one is small. The small village is under attack." (Notice that the smaller pueblo has an arrow point, and the bigger one does not.)

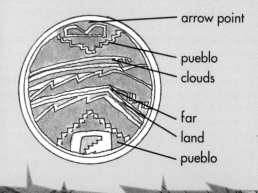

arrow point
pueblo
clouds
far
land
pueblo

WEAPONS AND HUNTING

Though their diet was mostly corn, Pueblos hunted and ate all sorts of animals: deer, mountain sheep, antelope, mountain lions, wolves, badgers, rabbits, foxes, even gophers.

Early Pueblos hunted with the "drive" method. A group of men—sometimes all the men and boys of a pueblo—would walk to where they knew there was game, surround the prey, and drive it to a canyon or a corral. There, they could easily kill it. Different animals required different techniques. For deer, one or two hunters would wrap themselves in buckskin and put antlers on their heads, acting as decoys while the other men drew closer. To stampede a herd of antelope, the Pueblos would howl like wolves, scaring the antelopes into a fenced area.

Large animals were scarce and hard to find, so the Pueblo men usually hunted rabbits. They rounded up groups of the little animals, which can run fast but not far. Rather than waste valuable arrows trying to hit a small target, the hunters clubbed the animals on the head. One type of rabbit club was curved at the end, so it bounced to one side or the other after hitting the ground. If the club missed its target, there was a good chance of it hitting a rabbit on the rebound. Sometimes, when the group of rabbits was thick, several rabbits were hit with one throw.

Traps were carefully laid, so that the slightest touch or tug on the bait would dislodge a stick and cause a trap door to fall on the animal. Stones were needed to weigh down a coyote trap, since the coyote is a fairly large animal.

Using the Whole Animal

Pueblos were appalled when they saw that white people used only a small part of the animals they killed and sometimes even killed just for sport. Indians used nearly every part of the carcass. Besides eating the meat, they made skins into blankets and drums, stretched tendons and intestines for bowstrings and thread, fashioned bones into tools and wall hooks, used rabbits' feet for paintbrushes, and even made hooves into rattles.

The Pueblos had great reverence for the animals they hunted. Dead animals brought back home were honored so that their spirits would not be angry. Deer often were covered with decorative blankets. Jewelry was hung around their necks, and prayer feathers were strung on the antlers. The Pueblos thanked the deer for giving their flesh so that the people might live, and they asked the deer to forgive the killers.

From ancient times, Pueblos used the *atlatl*, a spear-throwing device. On one end there was a place to rest the spear. The other end had straps that wrapped around the hunter's wrist or fingers. The atlatl doesn't look like it would do much, but by making the throwing stroke longer, it gave the thrower much more power. In the hands of a skilled hunter, it helped kill animals hundreds of feet away.

31

THE SACRED KIVA

In the middle of the pueblo was a room different from all the other rooms. It was larger and usually circular. And it was underground. The Hopi word for this place is *kiva*, which means "underworld." For the Pueblo Indians the underworld did not mean hell, but rather the middle of the earth, the place where people came from. The underworld was also the place where many gods resided.

On the floor of the kiva was a rectangular hole with a wooden cover. This hole, the sipapu, led from the underworld to the surface of the earth. *Sipapu* means "navel." Just as an unborn baby is fed through an umbilical cord leading to his or her navel, so the Pueblos felt themselves to be connected to the spirit world. The spirits could enter the pueblo through the sipapu to help the people.

Only men were allowed to enter the kiva, but the room served the whole community. The kiva was the center of Pueblo religious life, the place where the most sacred objects were kept. The walls were often painted with pictures that told sacred stories. The kiva also served as the dressing room for men who danced in public religious ceremonies. The dancers would climb from the kiva to the courtyard above to perform.

Being underground had religious meaning, but it was also practical. The kiva was cool in the summer and easy to heat in the winter. It was a good place for a men's club. Here men could practice the art of weaving. And here they spent long hours instructing boys in how to become Pueblo men. Stories and legends were told and retold, chants and songs were sung and resung. Boys could then pass them on when they became adults.

These kiva wall paintings may show prayers for rain and the goodness of the gods in granting it.

SACRED DANCES, SACRED DOLLS

P ueblo Indians have been called the "Rain Dance People." Pueblo people knew that their lives could be threatened at any time by lack of water. So a good deal of their religion—and religious dance—had to do with asking the gods for rain. But there was much more to their religion than that. Pueblo people told hundreds of stories about the gods and themselves. They revered the natural world. Their religious dances were great works of art, developed over centuries.

Pueblos danced all year round. Sometimes they danced slowly as they sang with deep voices, reflecting sadness at poor conditions. Other dances joyfully celebrated the growth of corn. Often dances told stories of various gods. Dancers wore elaborate masks and costumes. In one dance, the story of creation was retold. Dancers decorated with paint, branches, horns, and feathers emerged from the sipapu of the kiva. They represented gods, animals, and humans. In the snake dance, Pueblo men danced fearlessly with rattlesnakes. All these dances were carefully planned, but also included some time for people to dance freely. The dances often went on for hours.

Pueblos believed in *kachinas*—the spirits of animals, insects, plants, people, and even places. These godlike beings carried messages between gods and the people. They all had their own special personalities and purposes. Part of the year the kachinas lived far away in the mountains, and part of the year they lived in the pueblo. When a man dressed up as one of these spirits, he too was called a kachina, and the spirit was thought to live in his soul.

There were more than 250 kachinas, so it took plenty of homework for Pueblo children to learn about them. To help them learn, Pueblos made kachina dolls. These were carved out of wood, covered with white clay, and then painted in bright colors. Each was made to look like a certain kachina.

HEALERS AND CLOWNS

Pueblos had to spend most of their time gathering and preparing food and building shelter. But they also joined societies for special purposes and events. Rain-making societies specialized in prayers and dances to bring rain. Members of hunting societies knew the most about where prey could be found. Healers shared their lore with each other—they knew of more than 70 different plants that could be used for curing illness. Singers practiced and performed together. When someone died, a funeral society helped prepare the body and the burial site.

There were many ways to join such groups. A person could simply be born into a society: if your father or mother was a healer, you probably would be too. But if you had a special interest—in medicine or hunting, for example—you could sign up for membership in those societies. More than casual clubs, these groups often had secret rites and holy objects. You could even become a member by accident. For instance, if you accidentally touched the stick-swallowing society's sacred pieces of wood, you might be forced to join up!

We may not think that clowns are necessary, but down through history they have played important roles in many cultures. Perhaps people must learn not to take themselves too seriously if they are to survive. Among the Pueblos, members of clown societies impersonated important people and mocked them with songs. Clowns talked people into playing silly, childlike games, such as "Guess what I have in my hand" and "Guess which hand it is in."

Clowning often meant speaking and acting in a backward way. Clowns even mocked religious ceremonies. Clowns helped people forget their troubles and kept Pueblo society from becoming too strict and rigid.

The Final Journey

Pueblos respected old people for the wisdom they had gained over the years. When too old to work, a person would often become the head of a society or would join the town council. While the others were working in the fields, grandmothers and grandfathers taught children stories, training them in the Pueblo way of life.

Pueblos often prayed that they would live long enough to die in their sleep of old age. And they believed that when they died they would go to a place that was very much like this world. The only difference was that there, things would be backward: winter would be summer, and night would be day.

The dead were lovingly prepared for the next life by their relatives. The bodies were washed and dressed in their best clothes, their hair was fixed up and their faces painted. Then they were buried in a sitting position, with their most precious possessions next to them. Pots and plates were "killed"—that is, holes were punched in them so they could not be used.

Because of disease and difficulties in childbirth, many children died. The Pueblos felt the loss of their small ones deeply. The children were buried wrapped in furs. Often Pueblos would bury their children under the house floor. Because children were too small to make the journey to the next world, it was hoped that their souls would enter new babies born in the home.

Grave sites give us a helpful peek into everyday Pueblo life, because the dead were prepared for an afterlife that was much like this life. Archaeologists find ears of corn, bone knives, hairbrushes made of yucca leaves, seeds for planting corn and other crops, turquoise jewelry, charms to ward off disease, and other practical and beautiful everyday objects in Pueblo graves. Modern Indians dislike having their ancestors' remains unearthed and put on display in museums. Would you like it, they ask, if thousands of people came to stare at the bones of your ancestors? In recent years, archaeologists have learned to work more respectfully with Indian burial sites. The archaeologists put artifacts back in place once they have learned what the grave has to tell them. And many Indian remains that are now in museums are being reburied.

CONQUEST AND REVOLT

When the Spanish came to the Southwest in the 1500s, they were able to defeat the Indians with horses and superior weapons. They respected the Pueblos more than they did the other Indians, because Pueblos lived in houses and were farmers. But this did not keep the Spanish from treating the Pueblos cruelly.

The Spanish wanted to establish a feudal system in which the common people did not own their own land but worked for the benefit of wealthy overlords. The Spanish enslaved the Pueblos, forcing them to abandon their traditional religion. They made many people work in mines, while farmers had to give much of their produce to the conquerors. When Indians tried to rebel, the Spaniards did terrible things to keep them in line. Once, they captured 500 people and cut one foot off of each of them. Pueblos who refused to convert to Christianity were burned at the stake.

In 1680, after more than 80 years of this treatment, the Pueblos staged a revolt. This was not easy to do. The Pueblos were not one tribe but many different peoples who just happened to live in much the same way. They had never worked together before, and they spoke at least seven different languages. But they had a strong leader, Popé, who united the tribes.

Moving swiftly, the Indians took the Spanish by surprise and soundly defeated them. Pueblos brought out religious objects they had been hiding and sang songs that had not been sung in public for decades.

But the Pueblos preferred life as separate peoples, not as one united tribe. That left them vulnerable. And Chief Popé became a tyrant himself. Some Pueblos thought he was no better than the Spaniards. In 1692, the Spanish reconquered Pueblo territory.

The revolt of 1680 was one of the most successful attempts by Indians to gain back their traditional way of life. It failed, but not totally. In the following years, Spanish priests slowly allowed the Pueblos a little religious freedom. And in the centuries since that time, the Pueblo Indians have held on to many of their traditions, sometimes combining Pueblo religion with Christianity in their own unique way.

Pueblos and the United States

After the Spanish lost control of the area, the land of the Pueblos became the property of the United States government. Treaties were broken and white settlers took away some of the Pueblo land. But because much of their land was not considered valuable, Pueblos managed to keep more of their homes and customs than did many Native Americans. Modern Pueblos work hard to preserve their traditions and to make sure that within fast-paced American society, their heritage is not forgotten.

A Pueblo Recipe

Piki Bread

The traditional Indian recipe for piki called for cooking this paper-thin bread on a heated stone. The cornmeal was ground by hand on metates. A lamb's brain was used to grease the stone, and the only tool for spreading the batter and picking it off the stone was the cook's hand! This recipe is a good deal easier. A non-stick frying pan is a must. Have a parent or teacher help you.

For 8 scrolls of bread serving 4 people:

5 tablespoons Masa Harina, a finely ground cornmeal
2 tablespoons cornstarch
⅛ teaspoon salt
1 cup hot water

Mix the dry ingredients in a bowl, pour in the hot water all at once, and quickly stir the batter until it is smooth. Have a pastry brush ready. Heat a non-stick frying pan over low heat. It should not be so hot that the batter sizzles when you brush it on.

Take the pan off the heat and brush on a thin layer of batter, using broad strokes all in one direction. Immediately apply a second layer over this at right angles, in a crosshatch fashion. Do not worry about holes in the surface. Return the skillet to the heat and cook for about a minute. The batter has to sizzle and lose all its moisture before it is done. As soon as the hissing stops and the surface of the bread looks dry and crinkly, turn the pan upside down over a paper towel. Peel the bread off by turning up one edge with a table knife. The layer will peel away quite easily. Lay it on the paper towel—not on a plate. Make 3 more pikis and lay them on top of the first. You may have to rinse the pastry brush occasionally. If the batter thickens, add more hot water. Once you have 4 layers, roll them loosely and set aside. Serve slightly rewarmed or at room temperature with salsa.

VISITING PUEBLO SITES TODAY

Because Pueblo sites are often held sacred by Native Americans, visiting a Pueblo site is not like going to a museum or park. It is more like stepping inside someone's home where we follow the household rules—and use our best behavior. Here are some tips on visiting Pueblo sites:

Feel free to watch and enjoy the ceremonies and dances, but do not ask questions about the customs and beliefs. Pueblo religion has many secrets and mysteries. It is important to Pueblos that their stories and songs remain private. Pueblos do not like to answer questions about their ceremonies because there are seldom any easy answers. Their dances and songs tell long, complicated stories and have hundreds of characters. Often, the ceremonies deal with deep issues, like the meaning of life and death.

Sites to Visit

- Bandelier National Monument, north of Albuquerque, New Mexico (visitor center with Anasazi sites and petroglyphs)

- Chaco Canyon National Historical Park, northwestern New Mexico (Pueblo sites and petroglyphs, visitor center with museum)

- Hopi Indian Reservation, within the Navajo Indian Reservation in northeastern Arizona (includes old pueblos still inhabited)

- Mesa Verde National Park, near Durango, Colorado (Anasazi sites and petroglyphs, visitor center with museum)

- Santa Fe, New Mexico (Santa Fe Convention and Visitors Bureau will give information on museums in Santa Fe, as well as nearby pueblos)

- Taos, north central New Mexico (Taos pueblo, museum)

LEGENDS

The Gift of Corn

When the world was young, all people made their living by hunting, fishing, and farming. They had many crops, but they did not have corn.

One day, the star spirits decided to give people corn. But which people should be taught how to grow and use it? The star spirits assembled to decide this question. Moyachuntanah, the Great Star, proposed a plan. "Let us have a race," he said. "Each group of people will send its best runner. Whoever wins the race will win the gift of corn for his people."

The other star spirits liked this plan and agreed to it. So the three groups of people sent their swiftest runners: one from the pueblo of Zuni, one from the pueblo of Acoma, and one Navajo. (The Navajo are not Pueblo Indians, but they live in the same area.) Moyachuntanah took an ear of corn, broke it into three parts, and placed the pieces at the finish line. The tip was the shortest piece, the middle was a little longer, and the end was the longest. The winner of the race could choose whichever part he wanted.

At the starting signal, the three runners were off. They ran swiftly as deer. The people watched them excitedly, admiring their speed and hoping that their group's runner would win. The Navajo runner was swiftest, and he won the race. He chose the tip of the ear of corn, a surprising choice because it is the poorest for seed. Next came the runner from Zuni, who picked the middle piece. The runner from Acoma got the end piece.

Mokwanosenah, the Morning Star, who was brother to Moyachuntanah, said, "The Navajo has won the race. His people should receive the knowledge of corn." But Moyachuntanah, the Great Star, said, "It is true that the Navajo ran the fastest. But he chose the smallest piece of corn because it is the lightest and the easiest to carry. The Navajos will always wander from this place to that. They will never settle down long enough to plant and harvest. So his people cannot receive the prize. The Zunis and Acomas stay put and tend their fields well. So we will give them knowledge of how to plant and use corn."

And so it has been from the most ancient times. The Navajos continue to move from place to place and do not plant or harvest. They have a winter home in one area and a summer home somewhere else. But the Zunis and Acomas remain in their pueblos, and they make their living by farming. Corn is their most important crop, providing food to last the year round.

Why the Moon Has One Eye

The Kachina spirits, who are called the Trues, created T'hoor-id-deh, the Sun, to be father of all things. He was alone, so they made the first woman, Pah-hlee-oh, the Moon Maiden, to be his wife and companion. She had the seeds of all that was good and beautiful in humanity. All the world and all the creatures in it came from Sun Father and Moon Mother. They were full of joy as they watched their strong, happy children. Father watched over them during the day. Mother watched over them at night.

But there was no real night, for at that time the Moon Mother had two eyes. She could see as well as the Sun and was just as bright. There was unending day on the earth. Birds always flew, flowers never closed, people continually danced and sang. No one knew how to rest.

The Trues saw this was not good. The unending daylight lay heavy upon the young eyes of the world. Their tender eyelids needed soothing night. The Trues said, "Without sleep, the world is growing tired. We must not let the Sun and the Moon see alike. So let us put out one of the Sun Father's eyes. Then there will be darkness half the time, and his children will be able to rest." They summoned the Sun Father and Moon Mother and told them their plan.

When she heard, Moon Mother wept, thinking of her husband so strong and handsome. She cried: "No! For my children's sake take my eyes, and spare my husband! How will he supply them with good things? How will he protect them from harm or help them find game if his vision is darkened? Please, blind me instead!" The Trues said, "So it shall be, daughter." And they removed one of her eyes. Never again would she see as well.

Night fell upon the earth. This was good: the flowers, the birds, the people all slept their first sleep. And the Moon Mother, who sacrificed with pain as a mother will, did not grow ugly, but became even more beautiful. We all love her to this day. For though she lost the kind of loveliness that girls have, she gained the beauty that can be seen only in the faces of mothers.

> *So Moon Mother—soft with pale light,*
> *She bends, her loving watch to keep.*
> *With her sight she dearly bought the night,*
> *To give her children the blessing of sleep.*

Pueblo Terms and Their Meanings

adobe: building material made from clay and sand and applied like plaster; sometimes mixed with straw and made into bricks

Anasazi (Hopi word meaning "ancient ones"): people who lived in the Pueblo style

atlatl: a device that helps hunters throw spears with great force; used by Native Americans to hunt game

kachinas: more than 250 divine beings, believed to be the spirits of animals, plants, people, and places

kiva: center of religious life, usually in the middle of a pueblo, sometimes the largest structure in a Pueblo community

mesa: large hill or mountain with steep sides and a flat top

metate: grinding stone used for making cornmeal

petroglyphs: drawings carved in stone; made many centuries ago by the Anasazi

piki: bread made of paper-thin layers of fried cornmeal batter, traditionally cooked on a flat stone heated with coals and greased with lamb's brain

pueblo (Spanish word for "village"): a type of communal dwelling; used to describe many different Native American tribes

sipapu (Hopi for "belly button"): ceremonial opening in a kiva where sacred beings emerge to visit humans, in keeping with the belief that all life begins underground

INDEX

Steven Cory is a writer and carpenter living in Chicago. He first became interested in Pueblo Indians when his ten-year-old son saw their towns and wondered how they were built. Steven, who has a Ph.D. in religion from the University of Chicago, is also fascinated with Pueblo beliefs.

Richard Erickson graduated from Atlanta's Portfolio Center in 1989. A native of Chicago, he currently lives in the North Georgia Mountains with his wife Kathy, two sons, four dogs, and three cats.